GW00686125

NEW ZEALAND'S

NORTH ISLAND

IN COLOUR

NEW ZEALAND'S
NORTH ISLAND
IN COLOUR

PHOTOGRAPHS: MARTIN BARRIBALL
TEXT: MERVYN DYKES

Published by Reed Books,
a division of Reed Publishing (NZ) Ltd,
39 Rawene Road, Birkenhead, Auckland. Associated companies,
branches and representatives throughout the world.

ISBN 7900 0377 5

First published 1982
Reprinted 1986, 1987, 1989, 1992
This edition 1994

Cover design by Susan Johnson
Typeset by Jacobsons Graphic Communications
Printed in Hong Kong

Introduction

When the pioneers first encountered New Zealand's temperate climate, magnificent scenery and fertile soils they pronounced it "God's own country" — a land of wonders where crops and children grow with equal vigour; a land where steam and boiling mud and water burst from the ground and soaring glaciers made icy stairways to the sky; a land of opportunities for people prepared to work hard. New Zealand offered a new start; it was the new place to be.

People shaped this land to their needs with fire and steel; they gouged hills, erected concrete towers and slashing motorways. But for all that, their hold remained tenuous and the energy of their environment was such that nature could roll over their works in a few generations.

Men of legend tried to leave their marks in much the same way as more recent settlers. Maui, a legendary Maori hero, is said to have fished the North Island of New Zealand from the sea. His canoe was the older and more geologically stable South Island.

When they realised what lay before them, Maui's brothers raced on to Te Ika a Maui — The Fish of Maui — and hacked and carved out choice pieces for themselves.

The figures have passed into legend now, but the land remains: the larger South Island with its mountains, lakes, glaciers and wide-reaching plains; and the more populous North Island with its rolling green hills dotted with sheep and cattle, volcanoes, awesome thermal regions, bush-covered mountains and golden beaches.

From Cape Reinga at its northern tip to the capital city of Wellington in the south, New Zealand's North Island is a traveller's delight. The land holds an infinite variety of expressions and experiences. The people have dispositions as warm and inviting as the beaches of the Hibiscus Coast.

Some visitors race through the North Island on clockwork tours designed to cram as much as possible into the smallest capsule of time. Others go about their explorations at a more leisurely pace, stepping off well-worn tracks in search of the essence of the land and its people. But both groups will leave part of their hearts here and take something of New Zealand with them wherever they go.

This has always been so. The first explorers to visit New Zealand travelled half-way round the world to get here, spending months at sea in open canoes or sailing ships. Often they risked their lives in the process. They expected to find something different when they arrived, and they were not disappointed.

Some hundreds of years later that difference is still apparent, thanks to the strange timelessness of the Pacific. There is something hauntingly familiar about the country that will tease the deepest levels of memory. Is this North Island experience the way things were meant to be, with people and nature not too far removed?

We invite you to make your own voyage of discovery, either in person or through the pages of this book. We welcome you, but we warn you — you will never be the same again.

1. The Bay of Islands from the air.

2. Mount Maunganui, a popular resort for holidaymakers and surfers.

1

1. The rocky outcrop of Cape Reinga on the northernmost part of the North Island juts into the meeting-place of the Tasman Sea and the Pacific Ocean. It has special significance to the Maori people. Legend has it that from this point the spirits of the Maori dead part company with New Zealand and begin the long journey to their ancestral homeland of Hawaiki. But whatever one's race or personality, the atmosphere and sense of timelessness at Cape Reinga mark it as a special place for all who answer its call.

2. By their nature, lighthouses are usually found in lonely places. Erected as beacons to guide ocean travellers through troubled waters, they dot the headlands and harbour entrances around New Zealand's rugged coastline. The sentinel at Cape Reinga, however, has a unique distinction. Although it could lay claim to being the most remote, it probably receives more visitors than all the other lighthouses in New Zealand put together. Each year thousands of people trek to it so they can say they have touched one of New Zealand's boundaries.

3. Cape Maria van Diemen, looking back towards Motuopao Island. The cape was named by explorer Abel Janszoon Tasman who discovered New Zealand in 1642.

2

3

1. Part of the history of Northland and its people is preserved in what has become one of the premier tourist attractions in the area, the Wagener Museum at Houhora. The collection includes Maori artefacts, kauri gum, natural history exhibits, relics from early whaling ships and Victoriana.

1

2. The North Island is rich in beautiful harbours, but the attractiveness of Whangaroa, on the east coast north of the Bay of Islands, belies its bloody history. From here, Hori, chief of the local Maoris, led his warriors in a raid on the Wesleyan Mission at Kaeo, and it was here, too, that the notorious "*Boyd* massacre" took place. The *Boyd* was a timber ship which called at Whangaroa to take on kauri logs for Australia. In revenge for the captain's flogging of a chief's son, local Maori people guided a shore party to a place where they said some kauri could be found. They murdered the men and at dusk returned to the *Boyd* dressed in the victims' clothes. Once aboard, the Maoris spared only a woman and two children. The *Boyd* itself came to a savage end when a spark from a Maori pipe fell into gunpowder. Today Whangaroa is world renowned as a big-game fishing port and a place of peace and beauty.

3. Tane, the Maori god of the forest, still has some huge attendants in the Waipoua State Forest. One of them is the giant kauri known as Te Matua Ngahere, or the Father of the Forest, with a girth of about 17 metres. During pioneer days the kauri was much sought after for masts and spars. Its clean, hard timber also excelled for use in buildings that were meant to last. Once huge forests of these giants extended over much of the Northland peninsula. Now the few that remain are protected by law. It will be a long time before the forests return — if ever. After 500 years a kauri is still little more than an adolescent. Elsewhere in the Waipoua State Forest is Tane Mahuta, reputed to be more than 1,200 years old. The names given to these trees show the reverence in which they were held by the Maori — a reverence now shared somewhat belatedly by the Pakeha, their European countrymen.

2

3

1

2

1. The friendship between humans and dolphins is well chronicled back to the time of the ancient Greeks. However, in the summer of 1955-6 a touch of magic came to the beach resort town of Opononi near the entrance to Northland's Hokianga Harbour. Children playing in the surf were joined suddenly by a dolphin, which quickly struck up an amazing friendship. Opo, as she became known, proved a tireless playmate. She allowed children to ride on her back, played ball and tag with them, performed for movie and still cameras and generally brought with her a spirit of fun that captured the hearts of New Zealanders everywhere. Her death at the end of that glorious summer was an event of such sadness that a statue was erected to preserve her memory and to pay tribute to the gifts of friendliness she brought.

2. Further up the Hokianga is Rawene, a quaint old timber town. This view of the harbour was taken in that vicinity.

At once one of the oldest settled areas and most beautiful parts of New Zealand, Kerikeri nestles at the end of a narrow inlet in the northern reaches of the Bay of Islands. In the past it was home to people of two extremes — missionaries and marauders. Representatives of the Church of England set up a mission station there in 1819 and operated under the protection of the Ngai Tahu chief Hongi Hika. This same chieftain was the first in New Zealand to arm his warriors with muskets and in so doing was able to achieve a military supremacy over virtually all of the North Island tribes.

Today the name Kerikeri is synonymous with fruit and arts and crafts. Its orchards provide much of the country's citrus fruit, and in these pleasant surroundings, potters, artists and craftspeople of many persuasions have made their homes. However, reminders of the past are plentiful. Chief among them are the Stone Store at the Kerikeri Basin, now a museum, and the Kemp homestead, the oldest surviving building in New Zealand.

1

2

1. When the missionaries came to Kerikeri in the early 1800s, they built to last, whether it was in the spreading of the gospel or in the erection of more earthly signs of God's presence. A few metres from the historic Stone Store is a building commonly bracketed with it in tourist brochures — gracious Kemp House. Although it was built by the Reverend John Butler in 1822, Kemp House takes its name from a blacksmith and lay preacher, James Kemp, who occupied it 10 years later. Mr Kemp was one of the original mission workers and his descendants continued to live there until modern times. There are many unique features in the house's construction, and a tour is a rewarding experience.

2. If it is true that artists need peace and quiet to do their best work, it is hard to imagine a setting more inspiring than Kerikeri. There is a feeling of being close to nature and of energies more lasting than the fleeting sensations of the outside world. Potters, artists, spinners, weavers, workers in wood, leather and metal have been drawn to the district. Their roadside shops and studios tucked away in the bush attract a pilgrimage of art lovers who often have the advantage of being able to talk to the craftsmen and craftswomen at work.

3. Tales of sunken treasure have fired imaginations for centuries. For most people they remain tales, but at Paihia in the Bay of Islands there is the chance to see the real thing in a floating museum. Kelly Tarlton, one of New Zealand's best-known divers and treasure hunters, set up the museum to display the gold, jewellery and relics he has recovered from wrecks around the coast. Even the museum ship, the ***Tui***, has an interesting past. Originally a trading scow, it has been rigged with spars from a barque wrecked on a Northland beach. Now it serves as a major tourist attraction without leaving its moorings.

3

1

2

1. Who today could imagine Russell township as "the hell-hole of the Pacific"? Yet that is what it was called when, in 1840 as Kororareka, a wild whaling town, it was the largest European settlement in New Zealand.
In order to escape its licentious image the name of Russell was later conferred on the township, after the country's first "capital" a short distance away. But this did not spell the end of riotous activity there. Hone Heke, nephew of the famous fighting chief Hongi Hika, felled the British flagpole no fewer than four times in protest at British presence in the area. Heke's men then attacked Russell, sparing only the churches and mission buildings from their torch. These days the bays and inlets, seen here swathed in early-morning mist, are given over to deep-sea fishing boats and the occasional cruise ship. And Russell township? It's better known as a holiday and tourist centre.

2. The American author Zane Grey renamed the Bay of Islands "The Angler's Eldorado" when, in a book of the same name, he extolled the virtues of the fishing. Grey, an enthusiastic salt-water and fresh-water fisherman, made several visits to the area in the late 1920s and early 1930s. The reputation he helped establish for the Bay of Islands as one of the world's best big-game fishing grounds remains to this day.

BAY OF ISLANDS SWORDFISH CLUB
3-2-80
ANGLER TOM WILLIAMS
FISH 2 S/MARLIN
WEIGHT 68·5 90 kgs 150 lb 199
TACKLE 24 KG. B/S
LAUNCH LADY LOLA
Mobil
1

1. Here a striped marlin provides proof that the big fish are still biting in the Bay of Islands. In spite of the invasion by anglers from all over the world, records continue to be made. The skill and knowledge of the skippers and crews of the big-game boats is such that even a newcomer to the sport could end up with a trophy, a photograph and a tale or two to tell.

2. There is another kind of fish available at the Bay of Islands. Paihia carver, Joe Gamble, carves kauri reminders for unlucky fishermen and objects of art for those who appreciate the beauty of dolphins and fish.

3, 4. Fishing boats and pleasure craft at anchor near Russell.

2

3

4

1

2

3

1. Pompallier House, Russell, once part of the first Roman Catholic mission station in New Zealand.

2. A glimpse of Russell township from the hills behind.

3. This house on The Strand, Russell's picturesque waterfront, looks out over a peaceful bay in which whaling ships from around the world once lay at anchor.

1

2

3

1-3. A hui (Maori gathering) on the marae at Waitangi in the Bay of Islands.

4,5. Waitangi Day — part festival, part fun and part solemn commemoration. On 6 February 1840 Captain William Hobson of the Royal Navy and most of the paramount Maori chiefs of New Zealand signed the Treaty of Waitangi and founded a nation. Each year on 6 February this event is recalled in celebrations in front of the Treaty House, a beautiful old home where the original treaty was signed. Designed in the Georgian style, the house is open to visitors and annually thousands of New Zealanders and overseas tourists look through its rooms to sample a taste of history. Also of interest in the Treaty House grounds is the Maori Centennial Memorial meeting house or whare runanga. It is unique in that it contains carvings from many different tribes throughout the North Island instead of the usual set of carvings from a single tribe.

4

5

1

2

1. Travellers wait to board the ferry that will take them from Russell to Paihia. A variety of sightseeing cruises is available also, including the world famous "Cream Trip", a four-and-a-half hour cruise among the beautiful islands of the bay.

2. For those who like to see the sights at speed there's a faster alternative — a catamaran.

3. The catamaran lines up for its passage through the hole in the rock at Piercy Island, Cape Brett.

4. A view of the sights from the catamaran *Tiger Lily*.

3

4

1,2. One of the best features of the Bay of Islands is the large number of safe beaches which provide good swimming and easy launching for small boats.

3. Looking at the small wooden building that is Christ Church it is hard to believe that once hundreds of men swarmed around it locked in bloody combat. But a closer inspection provides proof in the form of bullet holes and the scars left by flying shot. The drama occurred when the Maori leader Hone Heke sacked the pioneer settlement of Kororareka, now Russell, putting to the torch all but the church and some associated buildings. Christ Church, built in 1836, is believed to be the oldest surviving church in New Zealand.

2

3

1. The principal centre of population in Northland is Whangarei city, situated on a beautiful natural harbour some 170 kilometres north of the metropolis of Auckland. Early records and Maori folklore indicate that it has always been a popular place to live. Safe anchorages, a river, forests, fertile soil, good fishing and a rugged screen of hills are only a few of the natural attractions Whangarei has to offer. The industrial life of the area is dominated by the Marsden Point oil refinery and oil-fired power station. Sheet-glass manufacturing and fertiliser and cement works are important, too, and counterbalance the attractions of Whangarei's congenial climate and proximity to the playgrounds of the "winterless" north.

2. Few cities can boast such an aquatic treasure as handy to suburban homes as the nearest supermarket. The Whangarei Falls are a delight whatever the season, and there is a choice of vantage points. The falls plunge into a narrow bush-covered ravine and are overlooked by a parking area at the top. The more adventurous can take easy bush paths to the foot of the falls for a closer view.

1

2

1

1. The towering Whangarei Heads which guard the entrance to Whangarei Harbour loom over the surrounding countryside providing a backdrop steeped in Maori legend. The drive from the city to the heads is a particularly rewarding one. The road winds through a series of small bays fringed with pohutukawa trees with flame-red blooms. Tiers of cottages are stacked along the hillsides. Several points offer excellent views of Marsden Point on the opposite side of the harbour, the bright-orange gas flare from the oil refinery acting as a beacon visible for many kilometres. Many of the bays offer safe swimming and boating.

2. What better place to go if you have time on your hands in Whangarei than the world-famous Clapham's Clock Museum? Named after a resident who began the collection, the museum includes a fascinating array of more than 400 timepieces from many parts of the world and several centuries. Children delight in the novelty clocks, but history buffs and lovers of beauty will be just as intrigued.

3. Muriwai Beach is beloved of surfers and fishermen throughout the north. Within easy reach of Auckland city, it is also a popular spot for picnics and family outings the year round. During summer, fishermen with long surf-casting poles try their luck for snapper and other ocean delicacies. The ocean is a wonderful playmate, but Muriwai should be treated with respect. Unwary fishermen have been swept from rocks and drowned. Swimmers are urged constantly to remember that the sea can be deadly and to swim within the areas covered by beach patrols.

2

3

1. Auckland is rich in beaches, and its North Shore particularly so. The notched eastern coastline offers a series of delightful bays almost at the front doors of the homes that press right to clifftop and water's edge. Browns Bay, in the foreground, retains its original village atmosphere, but has a major shopping centre screened from the beach by a thin line of trees and buildings. Mairangi Bay, four notches to the south, is similar. Even in bustling Takapuna city, just across the harbour bridge from downtown Auckland, the shoppers are less than five minutes from sand and surf. For a boat-loving, outdoors people the North Shore beaches are gems beyond price.

2. Mission Bay was once the scene of early missionary activity in Auckland. Today the district is one of Auckland's most desirable housing areas and comes complete with a lovely swimming beach and attractive fountain.

3. Just about everywhere one goes in Auckland, there is Rangitoto Island slotted snugly against the horizon. This symmetrical volcanic cone is the youngest of the islands in the Hauraki Gulf. Its name means "Bloody Sky" and is reminiscent of the titanic eruption that occurred when the island blasted itself out of the ocean little more than 700 years ago.

4. One of Auckland's best-known landmarks is One Tree Hill, here silhouetted against a darkening sky. The hill, like so many of the commanding sites around the city, was once a Maori pa and is now an extinct volcano. On the summit is the tomb of Sir John Logan Campbell, one of the founding fathers of Auckland. Reaching skyward with the tree that gives the hill its name is an obelisk erected as a tribute to the Maori people. Sir John's wooden cottage, built in 1843, is preserved as a museum at the foot of the hill in Cornwall Park.

5. An Auckland city sunset viewed from Okahu Bay.

2

3

4

5

1

1. After a hard week at the office what could be better than to hang from the trapeze of a sleek yacht as it cuts through the waters of the harbours and bays around Auckland? For those who like the sea, but do not have a boat of their own there are ferry and launch cruises around the Hauraki Gulf.

2. Love of the sea and sailing has reached epidemic proportions in Auckland. With ownership of a small yacht or power boat more popular than a second car, estimates of the size of the city's fleet of private pleasure craft range upwards from 50,000. Not only do some of the world's best sailors train on its waters but the city has also produced boat designers, sailmakers and boat builders of international ranking. The city has a choice of harbours to sail on and just beyond them lie the vivid blue waters of the island-studded Hauraki Gulf. Little wonder that the city's January anniversary-day regatta is the biggest in the world.

3. The yellow and black sails of a fleet of hire catamarans eager for flight offer a siren call to weekend sailors.

4. The marina at Auckland's Halfmoon Bay provides mooring and berthing facilities.

2

3

4

1. Sunlight tips masts and sails with gold in the Westhaven boat harbour.

2. Auckland's trademark, so far as works of people are concerned, is its "coathanger" harbour bridge linking the North Shore with the city centre. It also serves as the main route north from Auckland, connecting at both ends of its 1,100-metre span with a sophisticated motorway system. When the bridge was built in 1965 sceptics said it would never be used to capacity. However, its original four traffic lanes soon had to be doubled to eight, and it was joined by a second bridge further up the harbour. The developments with the harbour bridge (seen here looking towards the Westhaven boat harbour and the city) are symbolic of the rapid growth of the city. Auckland began rather shakily in 1840, enjoyed a brief period as the nation's capital and has since become New Zealand's biggest population centre with more than 760,000 people in its urban areas.

1

2

1. The face of downtown Auckland changes steadily. What was once one of the busiest intersections — that of Queen and Quay Streets near the waterfront — is now closed off by Queen Elizabeth Square. Nearby are shopping malls, hotels and a huge conference centre. This pedestrian plaza, with its strange sculpture capturing the essence of wind and water, counter-balances the civic square further up Queen Street.

2. In Auckland's early days Parnell was one of the most desirable of the inner suburbs. But by the 1960s it was a run-down ghost of former glories. The city was faced with the choice whether to restore or destroy. It opted for restoration, and the result — a shopping centre unmatched in New Zealand — won a national tourist award. It is a must for those who like to shop amid the charms of another age.

3. Quay Street on the Auckland waterfront is one of the most easily recognised parts of the city. To the left is the fringe of the downtown commercial area, and to the right, the Waitemata Harbour. The historic ferry building on the right in the middle distance, a reminder of bygone ages, is dwarfed by the newcomers across the street.

3

1

2

3

1, 2.The very name smacks of something special. Karangahape Road — sheer music the way it rolls from the tongue. But so much of Polynesia is music, and as Auckland is the world's biggest Polynesian city its multi-cultural charms come together like the instruments in a symphony orchestra. Karangahape Road forms the crossbar to a "T" that it makes with Queen Street in the very heart of Auckland City. It is a place of bargains and shopping surprises, and everywhere there is evidence of the South Pacific.

3.Costumed dancers celebrate at a wine festival in the "grape belt" — Auckland's western suburbs. Most of the vineyards were planted by settlers from what is now Yugoslavia. There are strong Croatian communities in both Auckland and Wellington. Others settled further north where they hunted buried deposits of valuable kauri gum.

4. Auckland is home to the world's biggest "fun run", the annual Round the Bays event which has drawn fields of more than 50,000 people. At quieter times, though, there are still joggers everywhere, and if the fabled runner's high fails to appear there is always the joy of the surroundings to compensate, in this case Mission Bay.

5. Parnell Baths — a large complex of saltwater swimming facilities near the Tamaki waterfront.

4

5

1

1. In the uncertain times after fighting in the Bay of Islands in 1845, the citizens of Auckland lived with the fear of invasion by hostile Maori tribes. Governor Grey established five "pensioner villages", forming an outer defensive screen overlooking the main waterway approaches to the township. In return for light military duties , former soldiers from the Royal New Zealand Fencibles were granted cottages on one-acre plots of land. Some 700 military settlers arrived and soon began to till their land, their labours supplying Auckland and ships in port with fruit and fresh vegetables. It is appropriate, therefore, that this former Fencible cottage in Howick, Auckland, should now be a restaurant. Known as Bell House, it caters to modern generations who come to dine in the shadow of the past.

2.The fittings in the cottages were simple by modern standards, but quite comfortable for people establishing themselves in a new land. Modern decorators often strive to recapture the pioneer look — the charm is undeniable.

2

3

3. The Polynesian collection at the Auckland War Memorial Museum is one of the finest in the world. The entrance is commanded by an impressive Maori canoe and meeting house that show to good advantage the artistry of those who fashioned them. There is an atmosphere about the exhibits that prompts reflection. For those who choose to sit on seats outside the meeting house and watch the reactions of the passers-by, there is a chance for some education in Maoritanga, too. At the push of a button, a taped programme explaining the history of many of the carvings and constructions runs tirelessly through its cycle of information. And the pakeha? Part of their history is upstairs in the equally intriguing Pioneer Street.

4. An aerial view of the museum which is set in the parklands of Auckland Domain.

4

1

2

1. Children and steam trains are a fun-filled combination. The Glenbrook Express, which runs on a special track south of the city, is a museum on wheels. Steam train enthusiasts come from miles around to ride the rails, and it's a winner as a family outing.

2. Carriage interior.

3. Auckland's Museum of Transport and Technology on the Great North Road boasts a working tramway among its attractions

3

1

2

1, 2. The big question at all zoos is whether the people are there to look at the animals or vice versa. Over a fence or in every cage or compound, there is an animal looking back, be it quizzical emu or haughty camel. Auckland Zoo is the biggest and best in the country, and a determined attempt has been made to provide attractions for children once they have seen enough of animals. The zoo is situated in a bush reserve at Western Springs, near one of the most magnificent museums in the Southern Hemisphere — the Museum of Transport and Technology. Both are on bus routes from the city.

3. The emblem of the north, the pohutukawa tree, provides a brilliant sight when it is aflame with blossom. Pohutukawas grow in stately avenues and cling by the most precarious of toeholds to clifftops throughout the north and even on the islands of the Hauraki Gulf. Their blossoms are usually red, although there are rarer yellow and white varieties. Maori travellers sighting New Zealand for the first time are reputed to have said: "Throw away your red feather head-dress; there are many red plumes dancing on the shore." Long may they continue to dance.

3

4

5

4,5. Fertile lands to the south of Auckland city provide much of its food from huge market gardens. In this instance the harvest is nothing to cry about, although the field is full of the best Pukekohe onions. Just over the back is the Pukekohe raceway, home to the New Zealand Grand Prix and international stars of motor racing.

1

1. All along the Coromandel Peninsula there are places where fishermen can try their luck or people can go to commune with nature. This delightful bay is located near Thames, the principal township in the area located at the foot of the Coromandel Range at the south-west edge of the peninsula. In the past people dug gold from Coromandel's hills. Today, one of the biggest industries is a happy reversal of this process — tourists flock to Coromandel in their thousands, bringing "gold" back to the peninsula communities.

2. Excellent sea views can be had from the fertile farmlands of the Coromandel.

3. Fishing on the rising tide at Whitianga on the Coromandel Peninsula. The district can boast a history of settlement going back more than 1,000 years to Kupe, the fabled explorer ancestor of the Maoris who is thought to have discovered New Zealand for his people about 950A.D. "Whitianga" is a contraction of "Whitianga-a-Kupe", or "The Crossing Place of Kupe". English explorer, Captain James Cook, was also familiar with the area, writing extensively in his journals of a place where the climate was gentle enough for people to sleep outdoors. The same qualities are appreciated today by people who have made it a favourite holiday spot.

2

3

1

2

3

1. Right in the heart of Hamilton is Lake Rotoroa (not to be confused with the similar-sounding Rotorua near the city of the same name). This lovely lake is artificial, but nature has accepted the assistance graciously and the area surrounding Hamilton Lake, as it is sometimes known, has become a playground. Yachts and rowing shells cut across the lake, and around its shores are picnic areas, a mini golf course, skating rink, swings, slides and everything else an adventurous child could wish for.

2. In the early days of New Zealand the Waikato River was navigable by ocean-going sailing vessels for many of its 425 kilometres. Now it has been dammed so often to provide hydro-electricity that much of it has silted up. However, it is still a thing of great beauty, this longest of New Zealand rivers, particularly where it flows through the booming provincial city of Hamilton. Actually, Hamilton has been booming since the late 1950s, but given the fertility of the surrounding countryside and the importance of the region to the country's agriculturally based economy, what could be more natural?

3. Rustling fields of maize abound on the fertile Hauraki Plains to the south of the Firth of Thames. Originally, much of the area was swampland, but drainage and skilled farming techniques have wrought dramatic changes.

1

2

3

4

1-3. The Waikato district is as rich in Maori history and culture as a chocolate cake is in calories. Nowhere is this more evident than at Ngaruawahia, home of Maori royalty and site of a thrilling annual regatta. Ngaruawahia is only a few minutes from Hamilton by car, and each March thousands of New Zealanders converge on the small township to enjoy the regatta and associated activities. They can see Maori war canoes glide by in the river, a sight Europeans might not have lived to describe little more than 100 years ago.
Then there is canoe hurdling, a combination of skill and fun. Canoes race up to and over log barriers set just above the surface of the water. For the unlucky this means a swim and for the conquerors a cheer from the crowds on the riverbanks.
Waikato is also home to one of New Zealand's most famous rowing clubs, the members of which have excelled in regattas as far away as Europe and North America. They, too, have their place in the Ngaruawahia festival. And everywhere, for everything that is done, there is an appreciative audience — even if some do have transistor radios to keep in touch with the outside world.

4. Not just one cave, but many, the Waitomo Caves are one of the world's major tourist attractions. Besides the weird and wonderful limestone formations there are glow-worm grottos that recreate the spangled beauty of the night sky. Waitomo (the name applies to the district as well as the caves) is 75 kilometres west of Hamilton. Regular tours of the caves are available and there is hotel accommodation nearby for those who take their time with their explorations. The glow-worms are of a different type to those found elsewhere in the world, apart from some distant relatives in Australia. To visit their haunt is to step into a place of enchantment.

1

1. Ocean Beach at Mount Maunganui, enhanced by the glow of dawn. While "The Mount", as it is known affectionately by most New Zealanders, is only 250 metres high, it gives a commanding view of the surrounding countryside. This fact was appreciated by Maoris who built a fortress on the site.

2. The Wairoa River near Tauranga offers plenty of thrills for those who like their water white, wild and woolly.

2

1

1, 2. Sunrise gilds the masts in the Tauranga Boat Harbour. Tauranga and its sister settlement, Mount Maunganui, together comprise one of New Zealand's most popular holiday areas, with whole cities of campers moving in each summer to take advantage of the temperate climate, pleasant beaches and fishing opportunities.

3. Situated just north of East Cape, Whangaparaoa Beach must have been a welcome sight to the Maori occupants of the canoes ***Arawa*** and ***Tainui*** who are said to have made landfall there after the long journey from Hawaiki. Fresh water cascades down to the beach for an added bonus.

2

3

1, 2. The East Cape of the North Island receives the first sun of each new day and all the world's capitals have to wait their turn. It's well worth the pilgrimage for those who like to be at the head of the line.

3. Waihau Bay is one of many popular East Cape camping places in summer. Here, and at the numerous other fine beaches and bays accessible from the East Coast Road, holidaymakers may enjoy the exceptional climate and scenery in relative tranquility.

4. The stamp of Captain James Cook is firmly imprinted on Tolaga Bay. Many of the streets in the small East Coast township are named after Cook, his ships or their crews. This reinforced concrete wharf testifies to a past as a bustling commercial port.

4

1

2

1. Just a short walk away from Tolaga Bay is Cooks Cove where, in 1769 and 1779, the master navigator refilled his water casks at what is now known as Cooks Well.

2. The city of Gisborne lies on the shores of Poverty Bay on the East Cape, midway between Tolaga Bay and the Mahia Peninsula. It was the site of the first European landing on New Zealand soil and has blossomed into a primary produce centre and starting point for holidaymakers.

3, 4. Board riders are of a breed that will travel many miles for the right set of surf, and remoteness is no obstacle to their enjoyment. Indeed, there is much more than surfing to enjoy in the solitude and beauty of such places as Mahia Peninsula. The peninsula is a stubby spear of land that thrusts southward at the northern extremity of Hawke Bay. Like many parts of the east coast, it has a long history of human occupation — by New Zealand standards, anyway!

3

4

1

1, 2. Nearly 206,000 hectares of rugged bush country make up New Zealand's easternmost national park. The Urewera National Park also contains beautiful Waikaremoana, the lake of rippling waters. The district is popular for its fishing, scenery and hunting. The Mokau Inlet is on the northern shoreline.

3. The reddish hue of rata flowers stains the bush near Lake Waikaremoana.

2

1

2

3

1. The Mokau Falls tumble over a 30-metre cliff, providing a constant attraction for passing motorists. The Urewera National Park is riddled with rivers and streams and there are several fine falls that are reasonably accessible.

2. Kereru, the native wood pigeon, is never far from berry bushes. A large bird with streaks of green and purple in its plumage, it is a surprisingly graceful flier.

3. The Hawke's Bay Aquarium at Napier houses an impressive display of ocean and tropical fish and tuatara and other reptiles.

4

4, 5. If animals have personalities the key trait of seals and dolphins would have to be a sense of fun. Not only do the ocean mammals at Napier's Marineland delight thousands of children and adults each year but they have a whale of a time in the process.

5

When Captain James Cook anchored off this point in 1769 a group of local Maoris tried to kidnap his Tahitian interpreter's servant boy. More than 200 years later this incident is recalled in the name given to the cape, which has earned fame for another reason — its bird colony. Cape Kidnappers is home to the only known mainland gannetry in the world. It is possible to hike to the sanctuary from the township of Clifton seven kilometres away, but many people take the alternative "safari" by four-wheel drive vehicle from the city of Napier on the coast further north. Cape Kidnappers is at the southernmost part of Hawke Bay, and part of the walking route from Clifton is along the beach. The gannets are the large white Australasian variety.

1. If it can be grown, it's probably grown in Hawke's Bay. The district vies annually with Nelson and Blenheim for the title of sunshine capital of New Zealand, and its market gardens yield prodigious quantities of fruit and vegetables. Nothing is more symbolic of the good life than a harvest of grapes such as these at Havelock North.

2. For those who like their grapes in bottles, the Te Mata Vineyard keeps open house. Visitors are able to sample the wares in the wine cellar surrounded by vats of red, white and true.

3. Even in Rotorua, the heart of New Zealand's most active thermal region, there is peace and serenity. This idyllic setting for the ancient game of bowls is in the Government Gardens not more than a few minutes from the city's main shopping district. Bowls is one of the most popular games in the country — some would say the most popular, in spite of the more robust appeal of rugby football.

1

2

3

1

1, 2. The ancient Romans were famous for their love of hot baths and the best in plumbing and central heating. So, too, were the Rotorua Maoris, but there are two important differences. When the Maoris arrived at Whakarewarewa the systems were already installed and they are still functioning today. Warm water bubbles up from the ground at temperatures ideal for bathing. Close at hand are boiling pools where the lady of the whare (house) can still cook food by dangling it in the water in a flax basket. Elsewhere in the city many homes are heated with the steam that squirts from rocks and fissures everywhere.

3. "Tread carefully all who come this way", could well be the warning from this carved figure at the entrance to a model Maori pa

2

3

near the Whakarewarewa thermal area, Rotorua. Although flimsy by the standards of the past, the pallisades give tourists an idea of the way things were when taniwhas lurked in the waterways and visitors who came calling might want more than a room for the night.

1

2

1, 2. However, when it comes to Pohutu Geyser only the foolhardy would want to get too close. There are seats set back a respectful distance for those who wish to wait for the geyser to blow its top. This it does several times a day, sending steam and water fountaining as high as 32 metres and often playing for more than half an hour.

3. At Wairakei, a few kilometres north of Taupo, huge clouds of steam billowing across the highway can make it look as if the earth has cracked open and an eruption is in progress. The noise and trembling ground seem to confirm this diagnosis. But relax, everything is under control. This is the site of the Wairakei Geothermal Power Station, which harnesses the energy of steam bores to produce electricity.

4,5. Between Wairakei and Rotorua lies the impressive Waimangu thermal district, which includes a large boiling lake known as the Cauldron.

3

4

5

1

1, 2. Some are bigger, higher, or prettier, but for sheer rock-trembling presence the Huka Falls are unmatched in New Zealand. Five kilometres north of Lake Taupo, the Waikato River is compressed suddenly into a 15-metre-wide rocky cleft about 230 metres long. At the same time the river bed falls eight metres as the torrent growls and jostles its way free of such impertinence. Finally, the seething mass of creamy blue-green foam spouts over the 11-metre drop of the falls proper and hammers into a deep bowl that has been scoured out over the ages. The water slowly loses its vivid colours as the river regains its composure and more realistic boundaries. The timid can view the spectacle from a loop road off the main highway. Those who are bolder can try a narrow bridge that spans the very brink of the falls.

2

3

3, 4. There is an old story about a tourist who arrived at his Taupo hotel in the dead of night and awoke the next morning thinking he was by the sea. This is an easy mistake to make because Lake Taupo, which extends over 619 square kilometres and is 160 metres deep, displays many of the moods of the ocean.

Taupo is an important holiday and recreation centre with a world-wide reputation for the quantity and quality of its rainbow and brown trout. For fishermen Taupo is the place to be, whether trolling from a boat off the mouth of the Tauranga-Taupo River, or as a "paling" in the celebrated "picket fence" where the Waitahanui River enters the lake.

4

1

2

1–6. With all that water around there is plenty of opportunity to indulge in aquatic pursuits of all kinds, or simply to relax around the lakeshore. The rivers and streams associated with Lake Taupo widen the scope of activities further, and canoeists are welcome on the Tongariro River — so long as they don't scare the fish!

3

4

5

6

1-3. Motorists on the main north-south highway always keep a lookout for the symmetrical cone of Mount Ngauruhoe (2,291 metres). They usually have plenty to see as Ngauruhoe grumbles and fumes away to preserve its reputation as the most continuously active of New Zealand's volcanoes. It is one of three major peaks in the Tongariro National Park on the central volcanic plateau to the south of Lake Taupo. While scientists clamber over the cone and even peer down its awful throat, they do so with a healthy respect. Tourists are left to admire the mountain from a distance or bestow their favours on Mount Tongariro (1,968 metres), 3 kilometres away to the north, or the twin-peaked Mount Ruapehu (2,797 metres), 16 kilometres to the south. A good place for admiring Ngauruhoe is from the vicinity of the Mahuia Rapids.

1

2

3

1

2

1, 2. Mount Ruapehu is the highest peak in the North Island and gets the lion's share of attention from tourists. It has fully developed ski-fields on several of its slopes and even boasts a hot crater lake surrounded by snow.

3. Here students at the Turoa ski school learn what fun is all about.

3

1

2

3

1-3. Tongariro National Park was gifted to the nation by the Maori chief Tc Heuheu Tukino IV (Horonuku) and other leaders of the Tuwharetoa tribe in 1887. They wished the sacred mountains to remain protected by their girdles of surrounding land for all time. There are many fine walks throughout the park, including that to the picturesque Tawhia Falls near The Chateau. Among the distinctive flora of the park is the umbrella fern and the native clematis.

4. Sheep graze on farmlands at the foot of Mount Ruapehu.

5. The Queen Elizabeth II Army Memorial Museum at Waiouru houses firearms, artillery, medals, insignia and uniforms used during military campaigns from the Maori Land Wars to Vietnam.

4

5

1

1. When it comes to superlatives, Mount Egmont is deserving. They all fit this central jewel in the Egmont National Park. An almost perfect volcanic cone rising abruptly from rich, green farmland is a sight that cries out to be photographed. The 2,518-metre peak has even been compared with Japan's Fujiyama, although the observer has to avoid the blemish of Fantham's Peak, an alternative crater bulging out of the southern slopes. Like Fujiyama, Egmont stands in splendid isolation. According to Maori legend he was chased there by the mountains of the central plateau when he paid too much attention to the charms of Tongariro's wife.

2. Taranaki, long famous for its pastures, is now rapidly becoming New Zealand's energy centre thanks to strikes of oil and natural gas. But whatever happens, Egmont will still be there to keep a watch over such modern-day attention grabbers as the Kapuni natural gas field and its flares.

3. In Maori mythology the legendary hero Maui hauled the North Island from the sea. Today the Maui natural gas platform, 34 kilometres off the Taranaki coast, produces new treasures. The gas is piped ashore to the Oaonui treatment station where it is prepared for its various roles. The gas reserves are expected to last beyond the year 2000, but with intense interest in exploration both offshore and onshore there is always the hope that there's more where that came from.

2

3

1
2
3
4

5

1. Ever since they were discovered in 1883, people have been coming to admire the Dawson Falls in Egmont National Park. Once they are there, a whole range of alternative activities opens up. Dawson Falls is now a resort area and one of the favoured starting points for climbers wishing to scale Mount Egmont. The falls are 18 metres high and were named after their discoverer, a postmaster named Thomas Dawson.

2. The Rangitikei River passes through some of the most rugged areas of the central North Island on its way to the sea south of Wanganui. The main highway between Auckland and Wellington carves its way through the hills nearby, as does the main trunk railway line, its course made easier by huge deviations and viaducts near Mangaweka. The river valley opens out into cliff-lined plains that are productive farmlands. The effect is wild and wonderful.

3. In rugged country waterfalls abound.

4. The Raukawa Falls are on the Mangawhero River, which rushes from Tongariro National Park to join the Whangaehu River north-east of Wanganui.

5. A tunnel of trees brings a touch of summer peace to the Parapara Road between Wanganui and Raetihi. This route follows the Mangawhero River for much of its course.

Rich in Maori history and as long on beauty as it is in kilometres, the Wanganui River is second in importance only to the Waikato in the North Island. Legends have it that the riverbed was carved out by Taranaki (the Maori name for Mount Egmont) as he fled the jealous Tongariro.

In the early days, the Wanganui was an important canoe route for travelling Maoris. Later, European settlers used a steamer service and today tourists still enjoy visiting the Wanganui's wilder places by leisurely launch, speedy jet boat or canoe. Bush-lined gorges on the upper reaches increase its air of mystery, but make voyages of discovery especially rewarding.

The township of Wanganui at the rivermouth dates back to 1840, the year of the signing of the Treaty of Waitangi. But there had been Maori settlers there for centuries. Today the "river city" is the centre of a thriving agricultural region to which come wool buyers representing clients from as far away as Europe. There are many pleasant drives in and around its environs.

1, 2. Students from many nations pass through this avenue of trees each year on their way to the Massey University campus at Palmerston North. Hailed as the most beautiful university in New Zealand, it specialises in agricultural sciences and often hosts international conventions and seminars.

1

2

3

3. Distinctive haystacks dot the farmland around the Rangitikei township of Bulls, midway between the cities of Palmerston North and Wanganui. The town's name comes from an English settler named James Bull who ran a hotel and store there. Bull, a noted carver, has examples of his work among the panelling in the House of Commons, half a world away in London.

4

5

4. The small Manawatu town of Feilding has an importance beyond its size. It is a service centre for surrounding farms which produce sheep, cattle and mixed crops. The big day of the week is sale day when the auctioneer is king and farmers come to buy, sell or just keep an eye on things. Less than 20 kilometres away is the major provincial centre, Palmerston North.

5. Sheep outnumber humans by nearly 23 to one in New Zealand. So far as the nation's economy is concerned, their fleece really is golden. About 75 per cent of New Zealand's export income is earned by agricultural products, and the farming expertise behind it is respected the world over. New Zealand is ranked among the top three trading nations in the world for meat, wool and dairy products. So what could be more typical than the sight of grazing sheep on a Manawatu farm?

1

2

1. New Zealand's 1,600 kilometres of often wild coastline took a heavy toll of early shipping. Part of the answer was a network of lighthouses established to save lives and assure the goods got to market. The Castlepoint Lighthouse on the Wairarapa coast still guards what for the pioneers was an important port, but the railways have taken its business away. Castlepoint continues to remind passing shipping of one thing that hasn't changed — the long fingers of rock that reach out to clutch the unwary.

2. The sloshing of surf and pounding hooves make a magical combination. Horse racing is one of the most popular New Zealand pastimes, and while racegoers have their Trenthams and Epsoms, beach meetings, such as this one at Castlepoint in the Wairarapa, have a special appeal.

3. Farmlands near Greytown were once part of an isolated rural community separated from Wellington by the Rimutaka Ranges. Now the railway lines punch through the hills — one of the tunnels being nine kilometres long — and a highway winds over the top. The Wairarapa farmlands still have their own identity, but Greytown, the oldest settlement in the area, is now only 80 kilometres from Wellington by road and doubles as a weekend retreat and even as a commuter base.

3

1

2

3

1, 2. The flaring fenders of a Bugatti a long way from home are one of many attractions at the Southward Museum, which houses some of the world's rarest cars. The museum is just north of Paraparaumu, an easy hour's drive from Wellington.

3. Silver-grey tiers of sand, surf and sky blend together as a solitary walker enjoys the serenity of a west coast beach near Wellington.

4. Who says beaches have to be sandy? The Makara Walkway, which skirts the edge of a rocky bay near Wellington city, demonstrates a charm of its own. There is good fishing in this vicinity.

4

2

1. Wellington harbour from Mount Victoria.

2. Named after its discoverer, Captain James Cook, the strait separating the North and South Islands of New Zealand contains some of the roughest ocean in the world. It is situated in the notorious "Roaring Forties" wind belt, and matters are complicated further by high land masses acting as a funnel for the gales. In spite of this the strait has many peaceful days and is a favourite testing ground for long distance swimmers. Inter-island ferries are popular both for strait crossings and day excursions. However, Barretts Reef on the western side of the entrance to Wellington Harbour was the site of the wrecking of the ferry *Wahine* in a storm in April 1968.

3. Putting best whiskers forward for the camera, a sea lion lolls among the curious onlookers at Red Rocks, south of the Wellington suburb of Island Bay. A few minutes further south at Sinclair Head there is a seal colony.

3

4. Parades of surf lifesavers are a common sight on the beaches in New Zealand and Australia. Surf clubs provide crack rescue teams, who polish their skills between rescues at surf carnivals and contests.

5. Beaches are focal points for animal and human activity in New Zealand. A line of red-beaked gulls waits patiently on a wall at Oriental Bay in downtown Wellington for crusts scattered by lunchtime sunbathers.

6. Even within the confines of Wellington Harbour there are many popular swimming and picnic spots. Scorching Bay is one of a series of pleasant notches along the eastern side of the Miramar Peninsula.

4

5

6

1

2

1. A typical Wellington scene — surburban homes stacked high on hillsides overlooking the Evans Bay boat harbour. With land at a premium in the capital city, every available home-site is used.

2. The main north-south highway merges with the Wellington Motorway and thrusts to the very feet of high-rise buildings in The Terrace, the home of big business in the capital.

3. Residential homes clinging to bush-clad slopes form the backdrop to this scene of Wellington's container shipping terminal.

3

1

2

3

1. Few visitors to Wellington leave without taking at least one ride on the cable car. The route climbs from the shops of Lambton Quay past Kelburn Park and Victoria University to the suburb of Kelburn. The park offers fine views of the harbour, and the final stop is near the famous Botanical Gardens.

2. Designed by the eminent British architect Sir Basil Spence, the additions to Parliament Buildings represent the centre of political power in New Zealand. Known as "The Beehive", the tower is linked to the older buildings in the complex which were modelled on the British Parliament at Westminster. In spite of its unusual design, The Beehive won speedy acceptance and fitted easily into the Wellington scene.

4

3,4. Dawn casts a golden glow over the city's commercial centre.

1

2

3

4

1. The other major centre of power in New Zealand is the game of rugby, in which leviathan forward packs churn through mud in pursuit of the elusive ball. No one is very certain whether rugby is a game or a religion here, but anyone can tell you that New Zealanders are world champions at it.

2. A colourful crowd of sports fans at Wellington's Athletic Park.

3. Members of the New Zealand Symphony Orchestra.

4. The amusement attractions at the Wellington Trade Fair provide fun for people of all ages.

Sunrise over Lyall Bay, Wellington.